P9-DGI-763

For my daughter Clementine, my mother, and my grandmother

Henry Holt and Company, LLC
Publishers since 1866
115 West 18th Street, New York, New York 10011
www.henryholt.com

Henry Holt is a registered trademark of Henry Holt and Company, LLC
Text copyright © 2003 by Frances Lincoln Limited
Location photographs copyright © 2003 by Oxfam GB and individual
photographers as named

Chocolate cookie recipe taken from *Happy Days with the Naked Chef*, p. 84
(Michael Joseph, 2001), copyright © Jamie Oliver 2001; reproduced in
simplified version by kind permission of Penguin Books Ltd., 80 Strand,
London WC2R ORL, England. Photograph of Jamie Oliver and children
reproduced by kind permission of David Loftus, copyright © 2001

All rights reserved. Distributed in Canada by H. B. Fenn and Company Ltd.
First published in the United States in 2004 by Henry Holt and Company
Originally published in the United Kingdom in 2003 by Frances Lincoln
Limited under the title *Let's Eat! Children and Their Food Around the World*
Illustrations by Anne Wilson
Designer: Trish Going and Sophie Pelham
Project Editors: Cathy Herbert and Susan Posner
Project Editors for Oxfam: Kate Hopgood and Anna Coryndon

Library of Congress Control Number: 2003104144

ISBN 0-8050-7322-1

First American Edition—2004
Printed in Singapore

10 9 8 7 6 5 4 3 2 1

Oxfam and the publishers would like to thank all the
children who took part in *Let's Eat!* and their families and
communities for their enthusiastic support. Oxfam and
the publishers would also like to thank the photographers
who were commissioned by Oxfam to spend time with
the five children featured in the book.

Toby Adamson visited St. Gervais in southwest
France to take photographs of Jordan. Then
he flew to Magdalena in Mexico to see Luis and
his family.

Jim Holmes traveled from his home in Laos
to Bangkok, the capital of Thailand, to take
photographs of AA.

Shailan Parker went to see Yamini and her
family in Kolkata, India.

Paul Weinberg took the photographs of
Thembe at home in her village near Durban,
South Africa.

Oxfam will receive a 5 percent royalty for each copy of this book sold in the United States.
Oxfam is a Registered Charity, no. 202918.

Oxfam believes every human being is entitled to a life of dignity and opportunity. Working with others
we use our ingenuity, knowledge, and wealth of experience to make resources and money work harder.
From practical work with individuals to influencing world policy we enable the world's
poorest people to create a future that no longer needs Oxfam.

LET'S EAT!

What Children Eat Around the World

BEATRICE HOLLYER

Introduction by JAMIE OLIVER

Henry Holt and Company · New York
In association with Oxfam

France: Jordan

I live in a village called St. Gervais, in the countryside. I have several favorite foods. I love garlic bread and oysters, but I don't like school lunches much.

Mexico: Luis

I live in a small town called Magdalena outside Mexico City. My favorite food is my grandma's homemade tortillas. You can use them to make enchiladas.

South Africa: Thembe

I live in the hills outside the east coast city of Durban, where it is warm and wet. My favorite food is Weetabix. I also like to chew on pieces of sugarcane.

OF FOOD

Thailand: AA

I live in the middle of busy Bangkok, the capital city. I love eggs so much, I eat them all the time. I don't like red hot chili peppers!

Contents

India: Yamini

I live in a big city called Kolkata. I have mangoes and watermelon every day in summer. My favorite dish is flat bread filled with potatoes and onion.

Chef Jamie Oliver and friends.

I don't know about you, but I've always been really curious about what other people eat. Being nosy is how I've got some of my best ideas as a chef—and discovered some of my favorite things to eat. This book lets you peek into the lives of five children around the world and find out what it's like to be them. If you live in Thailand, do you have to like chili peppers? Do they eat loads of weird stuff in other countries—or does everyone like popcorn, pancakes, and corn on the cob? Do all kids love sweets and ice cream as much as you do?

I love it that everyone has such strong memories of what they ate as children. This book is about those memories happening in kitchens all over the world. Imagine being these kids. Try out their recipes. Have loads of fun, like they do, smelling, touching, creating, tasting, laughing, and eating. That's what it's all about!

Jamie
x

Jamie's Chocolate Cookies

10 tablespoons unsalted butter • ½ cup sugar • 2 egg yolks • 2½ cups self-rising flour
2 tablespoons cocoa powder • 30 small pieces chocolate (milk, white, or plain)
two round cookie cutters, one about 1½ inches wide and the other about 2 inches wide

Preheat the oven to 375°F

Grease a large baking sheet. Beat the butter and sugar together until pale. Beat in the egg yolks, then the flour and cocoa powder. Turn out the dough onto a floured work surface, knead it, and put it in the fridge for 20 minutes or so.

Sprinkle the work surface with more flour, then thinly roll out about a third of the dough. Cut out 30 circles with the small cutter. Put a piece of chocolate in the middle of each one. Roll out the rest of the dough and cut out 30 circles with the bigger cutter. Put one on top of each chocolate piece. Press gently all the way around to seal the edges and keep the chocolate in. Bake for 10 minutes and eat hot or cold. Easy peasy, lovely jubbly!

SOUTH AFRICA

Rejoice Thembelihle Mthembu—Thembe for short—is eight years old. She lives with her grandmother, uncle, aunt, and three cousins in the green hills outside the city of Durban on South Africa's east coast. Thembe and her family don't have much money, but they always have plenty to eat because their crops grow easily in the warm, wet climate.

"My favorite food is Weetabix, but I don't get to eat it very often. I like to chew on a piece of *umoba* [sugarcane]."

Thembe's village has no electricity or running water. Most days, Thembe walks down to the bottom of the valley where a spring bubbles up through the rock into a pool. She carries the water back up the hill in a clay pot.

Thembe begins her day by helping her grandmother Gogo make a big bowl of *puthu* for breakfast. *Puthu* is a stiff porridge made from maize, which is grown in the fields around the village. Thembe shares the *puthu* with her uncle, aunt, and cousins. Her mother and father live with her father's family in another village. After breakfast Thembe walks across the hills to school.

"When I grow up, I would like a well-paying job so we can spend less time thinking about food."

At school Thembe does some weeding in the vegetable garden. The children either take what they grow home to their families or sell it to raise money for the school. Thembe thinks working in the garden is important but boring—she would rather be cooking.

7

After school Thembe collects some firewood and builds a fire underneath the cooking pot. Sometimes Gogo asks her to climb the lemon or mango tree to pick fruit. Today she needs mealie meal (cornmeal), so she asks Thembe to walk to the grocery store.

On the way home Thembe carries the mealie meal on her head. If she really concentrates, she can do it without holding on. All the women in Thembe's village carry firewood and water this way.

"I like looking at the chips and sweets in the shop. Now and then Gogo has some spare change and lets me buy some."

8

Thembe starts dinner by boiling the mealie meal to make *puthu*. She knows how to cook most things and only needs help to prepare a whole meal. Tonight's dinner is her favorite: beef grilled above the cooking fire, with barbecued mealies (corn on the cob), *madumbes* (a root vegetable like a potato), *puthu,* and *amasi* (sour milk), which they have as a sauce and as a drink.

The *puthu* is served first to fill them up and make the meat go further. Thembe piles the *puthu* into a bowl with some vegetables and sits down to share it with her cousins. Children, men, and women all eat separately, using their fingers, according to Zulu tradition. As she scoops up the food, Thembe chatters excitedly with her cousins about the big wedding party planned for the next day.

A special day for Thembe's family—a wedding

The next morning Thembe helps her aunt Ntombi tie her best skirt and shawl and put on a special headdress for the wedding. Thembe wishes she was going as well, but she has a large family, so her aunt and uncle are going to represent them all.

The bride and groom, who are both related to Thembe, have saved up for a traditional wedding. According to Zulu custom, even if money is short, there must be plenty of food and drink for everyone. Before they leave, the bride's friends pin gifts of money to her headdress. Then they walk in a procession to the groom's village.

When they arrive, the bride's brother dances and sings a story about their family. He acts it out with sticks and shields made from animal skins.

The children at the wedding think the dancing is the most exciting part of the day. Like Thembe, they love dressing up in beaded headbands, belts, and necklaces.

"There will be Coca-Cola and orange soda at the wedding feast, and a special pudding made with condensed milk. I hope my aunt will bring some back for me."

The groom's friends have killed two cows for the wedding feast. The best pieces are barbecued for the men, and the rest is put into big pots to stew. The meat is served with soft, doughy bread, which is steamed on top of the meat in the pots, and lots of different salads.

After a long day of singing and dancing, the guests feast and celebrate late into the night.

MEXICO

Luis Emanuel Sánchez Jiménez is six. His family's pet name for him is Guicho, but his teachers call him Emanuel, which he likes better. He lives in a small town called Magdalena between the countryside and Mexico City. Mexico City is one of the world's most populous cities.

Magdalena is high up, so the air is fresh and cool. From the church you can look down into the valley. Magdalena was once a farming village. Now most people who live there go to work in the city every day. Luis's father drives them there and back in his bus.

Luis lives in a two-room house with his parents and sister. His grandparents farm a small plot of land nearby. They grow corn and keep sheep and chickens. Luis enjoys collecting eggs and seeing how food grows, but what he likes best is learning to look after the sheep.

When Luis gets up in the morning, he washes his face with water from a big cement basin in the courtyard. Then he has some cold rice pudding or cornflakes, and chocolate milk. His school has running water, so he brushes his teeth there after the morning snack break.

"I have juice and a cake at school, but sometimes I don't eat it because I want to go off quickly and play with my friends."

Luis is too excited to eat his cake today. It is the start of the Christmas holidays, and his parents are coming to see him perform in the class Nativity play. While Luis waits his turn, he watches his classmates tell the story of "El Burrito de Belen," a small donkey who travels to Bethlehem.

Luis carefully carries his gold paper crown as he leaves school with his mother and his little sister, Ana. They are going to have a holiday lunch with his grandparents. On the way, they shop for food. They do this every day, because they don't have a fridge at home.

"I am always asking Mom to peel an orange for me. I like to suck the sweet juice out."

Luis and Ana enjoy helping their mother decide what to buy. At the bakery Luis chooses a cake for after supper. Then they go to the tortilla makers for some tortillas. They eat tortillas at nearly every meal. Luis's mother buys them by the pound, but his grandmother makes her own. Their last stop is the vegetable market, where they buy some fat cactus leaves for a special salad made with cilantro and salt.

As soon as Luis arrives at his grandparents' house, he hurries to feed the sheep and herd them into the small pasture. While he helps his grandfather with the animals, his grandmother cooks tortillas on the fire. She makes them with corn she grows herself. Luis thinks her homemade tortillas taste much better than the store-bought ones he has at home.

A special day in Luis's life—fiesta

Just before Christmas, Luis visits his other grandparents for a fiesta (festival) to celebrate their town's patron saint. Everyone gets up early for church and fireworks, then they come home for a big family brunch. Luis eats sweet bread, although his mother encourages him to try some scrambled egg, refried beans, or fish soup. There are piles of hot tortillas on the table.

**"My favorite food is tacos
with tuna fish or cheese.
I can eat six of them at one meal!"**

Luis likes to eat his tacos with a spicy tomato salsa (sauce). His grandmother makes it with chopped tomatoes, onions, green chilies, and cilantro. She also adds a pinch of salt and a squeeze of lime juice.

As night falls, Luis's mother and father take him and his sister to the fairground in town. The streets have been decorated with flowers and streamers. People crowd around stalls that sell every kind of food and drink. Luis chooses a taco from one stall, then an ice cream with fresh fruit from another.

Luis stays up very late to enjoy the fiesta. The best part is the fairground rides, although they whirl him around so fast he's glad his father is holding on to him. He's looking forward to two more days of celebrations and feasting before he goes home to Magdalena for Christmas.

THAILAND

Kamalotas Sudasna lives in Bangkok, the capital city of Thailand, with her mother, father, grandmother, and brother. Everyone calls her by her nickname, AA. She is eight, and her brother, Sutaspong, is three. AA prefers plain food to traditional spicy Thai dishes. She especially avoids red chili peppers, which are used in cooking to add a fiery flavor.

AA enjoys going to the supermarket with her family to buy rice and other packaged food. Like most people in Bangkok, they buy fish, meat, vegetables, and fruit every day at the local market or from street vendors who walk into the city in the early morning.

AA's grandmother Khun Yai does all the cooking for AA's family, including her uncles, aunts, and cousins, who live in the same building. Today Khun Yai has bought some steamed rice from a street vendor on her way back from the market. AA and her cousin have some for breakfast with AA's favorite dish, *khai jiow moo supp*—Thai fried eggs.

"I love eggs. I eat them all the time, at nearly every meal."

A monk from the nearby temple comes to AA's house every morning. AA feels special when it is her turn to give him the food her grandmother has prepared. Her family are Buddhists, and supporting the monks who study at the temple is an important tradition for them.

Sometimes AA cooks her favorite Thai fried eggs herself. She shakes some salty soy sauce into the beaten egg mixture to make it more tasty.

After school, while her mother and father are still at work
in their offices, AA goes to the market with her grandmother
to shop for dinner. Khun Yai is teaching AA how to choose the
freshest fish, the ones with bright eyes and red gills. They get some
pork at the butcher's stall, some quail eggs, then some greens.
AA and Khun Yai take turns carrying the heavy basket.

Back at home, AA is in charge of cooking the quail eggs for dinner. While her father builds up the fire in a small charcoal stove in the courtyard, AA puts oil in the holes of a special egg pan so that the eggs won't stick. Then she breaks a quail egg into each hole and covers it with a little terra-cotta lid while it cooks.

"Mom or Dad always watches to make sure I don't burn myself, but I am really good at cooking eggs and I never do."

Dinner always includes a big bowl of rice. Khun Yai used to cook it in a clay pot, but now she has an electric rice cooker. Tonight there are six other dishes, including several different vegetables. AA eats lots of rice, but she says the vegetables are too spicy.

A special day in AA's life—a day out with Dad

Today is Saturday, and AA is excited because she is going to spend the whole day with her father, Kittima. They set off on their bicycles, riding around the park near the temple. It is a peaceful place, away from the noise and traffic fumes of the city center.

They stop at a stall that sells drinks and ices made from fruit syrups. AA chooses strawberry-flavored crushed ice with a topping of icing sugar. The ice melts quickly in the sun, and AA sucks up the cold, sweet liquid with her straw.

"Next time I'll have durian ice cream. The fruit smells funny, but the ice cream tastes good!"

AA and her family are friends with the Thai-Chinese family who run the local noodle shop. There are three types of noodles to choose from, with different sauces and toppings. Kittima has flat noodles with slices of cuttlefish, green onions, and chili sauce. AA likes the thin noodles in soup. She doesn't want her day out with Dad to end, but they have fun planning the route they will take on their ride home.

FRANCE

Jordan Pignier is eight years old. He lives in a village called St. Gervais, in the Limousin region of southwest France.

Jordan's father and mother, Jean-Marc and Geneviève, own a bar and restaurant. People come for breakfast, lunch, and dinner, as well as in between for drinks and snacks. Jordan often works in the kitchen with his father and helps his mother look after the guests.

"My favorite things to eat are hamburgers, steak, fries, chicken, garlic bread, and chocolate cake. Oh, and oysters."

On weekends Jordan loves climbing trees in the forests outside his village. He usually says hello to a herd of Limousin cattle on the way. People visit Limousin from all over the world to enjoy the good cooking and the beautiful countryside.

Jordan has his breakfast in the bar. He dips his *pain au chocolat* (flaky pastry filled with chocolate) or some baguette (long, thin bread) with chocolate spread into hot chocolate served in a special breakfast bowl. He finishes quickly so that he'll be in time for the school bus when it stops outside the restaurant.

"I get up late and rush my breakfast on school days, but on weekends I wake up early so there is more day for me!"

School lunch today is vegetable soup, then turkey with peas and carrots, then fruit and cheese. The children have a different three-course meal every day. Breakfast is always a light meal in France, so lunch is important, and Jordan is hungry. Today he eats the soup and the turkey, but he thinks the peas and carrots are too mushy. Jordan likes his father's cooking much better. He also prefers to eat at home because it's not so noisy!

When he has finished his homework, Jordan makes a chocolate cake. He doesn't need a recipe. He breaks eggs into a bowl, adds cocoa powder, yogurt, flour, and butter, then tastes to check. He thinks the mixture needs more sugar. Once he is sure it's perfect, he butters a baking pan and puts the cake into the oven.

"When I grow up, I might be a fireman, a doctor, or a chef."

While his cake is baking, Jordan helps prepare for dinner in the restaurant. He cuts the baguettes with a special slicer and carries a basket of bread to each table. Everyone eats lots of bread, so the baskets are refilled throughout the evening.

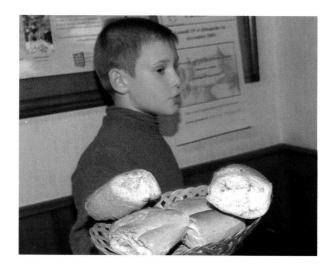

Before the guests arrive, the family have their own dinner. Jordan likes oysters because they taste of the sea. He enjoys cutting the oyster from its shell and scooping it into his mouth. His father has opened twelve for each of them.

"Oysters are good for you!"

A special day in Jordan's life—mushrooming

Early on Saturday mornings in the autumn, Jordan and his father, Jean-Marc, go hunting for mushrooms. Each time they go, Jordan learns a bit more about the different types and how to tell them apart. He knows that there are some you shouldn't pick because they are poisonous.

"I started looking for mushrooms when I was young— I don't remember when."

The best mushrooms they find are called cèpes. Some of them are as big as plates. Jordan is very pleased when he finds one small and four large cèpes.

Jordan is learning how to clean the mushroom stem by stripping the outer skin with a knife. He puts the pieces of mushroom that he cuts off back on the ground and covers them with moss so they will grow into new mushrooms next year.

Back at home, Jean-Marc cooks the mushrooms in butter. Jordan has some for dinner with steak and potatoes. He is proud that, thanks to him, the restaurant guests will enjoy a special treat tonight.

"We have been to mushroom paradise!"

INDIA

Yamini Arora lives with her parents, sister, and grandparents in Kolkata, one of India's biggest cities. Until 2001 it was known as Calcutta. Yamini and her older sister, Soheni, are named after ragas, which are forms of Indian classical music.

From her home in a tall apartment building, Yamini can see the Hugli River, which runs through the center of the city. Lots of people take the ferry across the river every day to go to work. The Howrah Bridge, which was made in the United Kingdom, is a famous landmark.

Yamini's grandmother, whom she calls Amijee, helps to cook and care for the family. Yamini adores Amijee and loves to spend time shopping and cooking with her. As soon as she wakes up she goes to find Amijee for a cuddle.

Yamini has a light breakfast because school starts very early in the morning. She drinks a big mug of milk and eats a few cookies, which she likes to share with her grandfather, Dadu. Some days she eats a bowl of chocolate cereal flakes. On weekends, when there is more time, she has toast and sometimes an egg.

On the way to school with her mother, Yamini sees a street vendor selling guavas and stops to buy one. She will eat it for tiffin, her snack at school break. Yamini likes to eat fruit every day, especially mangoes and watermelon in summer. In winter she has guavas, bananas, papayas, apples, oranges, or berries.

"Today for tiffin I've got popcorn, cucumber, guava, and a cookie. Sometimes I don't like my tiffin and I give it to the birds."

When school is over, Yamini and her sister come home for lunch. Yamini chops carrots to eat raw with cucumber. She is not allowed to fry the *puris,* a kind of puffed bread, because the oil is too hot. She can't wait for them to be ready. Yamini likes to eat *puris* with chutney and *dal,* a sauce usually made from lentils. After lunch she cooks a coconut dessert called *naryal ladoo*.

Yamini enjoys shopping for food in the market. It's called New Market, although it's in one of the city's oldest buildings. Before she goes inside, Yamini chooses vegetables from a street vendor's stall for her favorite dish, *aloo paratha,* flat bread filled with potatoes and onion.

"Once I saw a chicken killed at the market.
The man pulled a chicken with black feathers
out of his basket, then he chopped off its head."

The grocery stall sells dried lentils and chickpeas for *dal,* colorful spices, and several different kinds of rice. Yamini likes the delicate flavor of basmati rice. Today is Tuesday, vegetarian day for the whole family. For dinner they have rice, *chapatis* (flat bread), chickpea *dal,* vegetables, and *paneer,* which is a freshly made cheese. It's past nine o'clock when dinner is over, and Yamini is ready for bed.

A special day in Yamini's life—her birthday

On her seventh birthday, Yamini's mother gives her a soft toy cat. Yamini names it Hibiscus, after the red trumpet-shaped flowers in the roof garden of their apartment building. Then her sister helps her to pack a picnic. Yamini chooses her favorite snacks—cheese sandwiches, cookies, and pineapple. Amijee has also made *halwa,* a special dessert with almonds that she makes for everyone's birthday.

"I always have a cake with candles and jelly, and *fryums,* deep-fried soybeans colored red, blue, green, and yellow."

Yamini and her mother enjoy the sunshine in the park before their picnic. Then they unpack the *halwa* from its decorated box, and Yamini pours homemade lemonade. Her mother makes it by squeezing lemons and adding sugar and water to the juice. She leaves the mixture in the sun until the sugar dissolves.

Yamini is looking forward to joining in the preparations for her birthday dinner. Amijee is making a cake, cookies, and jelly-jujus (jelly candies covered in sugar). On the way home, they stop at Yamini's favorite cookie shop, and her mother lets her choose whatever she wants. Yamini gets a cake for her grandfather, too. He likes sweet treats as much as she does.

RECIPES

Try some of the children's favorite dishes for yourself.
You can buy all the ingredients you need from a local supermarket.
Remember to ask an adult for help before using the stove, the oven,
a hot pan, or a knife.

Thembe's Condensed Milk Tart

This is a kind of custard tart, called *melktert* in South Africa. Thembe's version doesn't need baking. It's quite sweet, which is why she likes it.

1 seven-ounce package plain butter cookies
1 tablespoon butter or margarine
1 fourteen-ounce can condensed milk
3⅓ cups warm water
½ cup cornstarch
⅓ cup cold water
1 teaspoon vanilla extract
2 medium eggs
Cinnamon (optional)

Set a few cookies aside and arrange the rest in an overlapping layer in the bottom of a 2-inch-deep baking dish. Put the butter or margarine into a saucepan with the condensed milk and warm water and stir over low heat until smooth.

In a separate bowl, whisk together the cornstarch, cold water, vanilla, and eggs. Then add this mixture to the saucepan and cook gently for about 10 minutes.

Slowly pour the mixture over the cookie base. Crush the reserved cookies and scatter the crumbs over the top. Add a dusting of cinnamon, if you like.

Put the tart in the fridge to set for a couple of hours before serving.

36

Luis's Tomato Salsa

You could try this delicious tomato relish with beans and rice, with fish sticks, or with burgers and sausages at a barbecue. It would be especially good as a dip with tortilla chips or pita bread.

4 large or 6 medium-size ripe tomatoes • 2 small onions • 1 bunch fresh cilantro
2 green chili peppers • 1 teaspoon sugar • Pinch or two salt • 1 lime

Finely chop the tomatoes and onions and mix together in a bowl. Roughly chop the cilantro leaves and add. Cut open the chilies and scrape out the seeds; wash your hands immediately after doing this because the pepper oil can sting. Finely slice the chilies and mix with the other ingredients, along with the sugar, salt, and a sprinkle of lime juice. Leave the salsa to stand for about 30 minutes before eating so the flavors have time to combine, then serve.

You don't need to stick to exact quantities for this recipe. You might find you prefer more or less salt or lime juice; it's up to you. A little sugar helps to bring out the taste of the tomatoes. And if you don't like chili, just leave it out!

AA's Thai Fried Eggs

AA eats her eggs with rice, but they would taste just as good with bread or fries—or bacon. Remember, the frying pan will get hot. Ask an adult to help you.

2 large eggs • 1 teaspoon fish sauce (available at Asian grocery stores)
1 teaspoon soy sauce • 1 tablespoon water
2 green onions • 1 tablespoon vegetable or sunflower oil
Fresh cilantro leaves (optional)

Whisk the eggs together with the fish sauce, soy sauce, and water. Finely chop the green onions and add them to the egg mixture. Then heat the oil in a frying pan or wok until very hot. Slowly pour in the egg mixture. When the egg begins to brown underneath, flip it over with a spatula and cook the other side. Slide it onto a plate and garnish with cilantro.

Jordan's Chocolate Cake

Jordan makes this cake without a recipe because he has done it lots of times. The unusual ingredient is yogurt, which makes the cake moist and light. You could use buttermilk instead. Remember to ask an adult to put the cake into the oven and take it out. It tastes delicious with vanilla ice cream or spread with cream cheese.

2½ cups all-purpose flour
1 tablespoon baking powder
1 teaspoon baking soda
14 tablespoons unsalted butter, softened
⅞ cup sugar
2 eggs
2 teaspoons vanilla extract
⅝ cup cocoa powder
1 cup plain yogurt

Preheat the oven to 350°F

Lightly grease an 8-inch round cake pan.

Sift the flour, baking powder, and baking soda into a bowl and set it aside. In another bowl, cream together the butter and sugar. Add the eggs and vanilla and beat lightly until combined. Sprinkle in the cocoa, then pour in the yogurt and mix well. Add the flour mixture and fold it in lightly.

Spoon the batter into the greased pan and smooth the top. Bake for 1 hour, until a metal skewer (or knife) inserted into the center of the cake comes out clean. Don't worry if the top of the cake is cracked.

Let the cake cool for a while in its pan before turning it out onto a wire rack.

Yamini's Coconut Sweet

In Hindi, the language Yamini speaks, this recipe is called *naryal ladoo* (*naryal* means "coconut"). *Naryal ladoo* is very easy to make. Yamini makes it after lunch and eats it right away.

To try *naryal ladoo* for yourself, you'll need to buy a fresh coconut from a vegetable market or grocery store. Ask an adult to break it open for you, then pour the cloudy coconut water into a jug and save it for another use. It's good to drink, or you can add it to a curry.

Cardamom is a fragrant spice, used a lot in Indian cooking; you can find it on the spice shelves at the supermarket.

1 large coconut
1 cup sugar
½ teaspoon ground cardamom

Once you have poured the water from the coconut, ask an adult to chop it into chunks for you. Using a coarse grater, grate the white flesh into a bowl. Then put the sugar into a frying pan or wok and heat it until it starts to melt. Be careful—the sugar syrup will be very hot. Add the grated coconut and cardamom and stir until the mixture sticks together and turns a light golden-brown. Turn off the heat and keep stirring as the mixture cools.

When you are sure the mixture is cool enough to touch, pinch off small pieces and roll them into balls about the size of a walnut. Put them on a plate and leave them to cool completely before eating.

Food Glossary

South Africa

amasi Milk left to curdle and go sour. Many Zulu people prefer *amasi* to fresh milk.

madumbe A root vegetable that is similar to a potato. It is also known as taro.

maize Another word for corn: long white or yellow spears of grain that grow inside tall, leafy plants. In South Africa maize is a staple food (which means it is eaten every day).

mealie meal A rough, white flour made from ground maize. It is cooked to make *puthu*, which is very filling and cheaper than rice or potatoes.

umoba Sugarcane, a tall grass that is grown as a crop. The sweet syrup inside the cane is extracted to make sugar.

Weetabix A whole-grain breakfast cereal from the United Kingdom.

Mexico

cilantro An herb (also known as coriander) that looks similar to parsley but has a spicy smell and flavor. The seeds are also used in cooking.

refried beans Dried beans, first cooked in water, then mashed and fried.

sweet bread Light bread, like cake, eaten for breakfast or snacks.

taco A soft corn tortilla wrapped around a warm filling of meat, fish, or cheese.

tortilla A thin, round flat bread, usually made from corn, eaten at nearly every meal in Mexico.

Thailand

cuttlefish A sea creature that resembles a squid, but has a broader body. Like squid, cuttlefish produce dark brown ink, which is used in cooking, as are the body and tentacles.

durian A large, spiky tropical fruit with pale green skin. The creamy flesh inside smells rotten but has a fresh taste.

fish sauce A salty, strong-tasting sauce made from fermented fish.

quail eggs The delicate-flavored eggs laid by quails. Quails are small, short-tailed game birds and are also good to eat.

rice The main crop of Asia, grown in flooded fields called paddies. Rice is a type of grass; the grains of rice are the plant's seeds.

soy sauce A salty brown sauce made from fermented soybeans.

France

baguette A long, crusty white loaf of bread. French people buy fresh ones every day.

cèpe A large wild mushroom with white flesh and a rich, woody taste. In Italy, cèpes are called *porcini*.

oyster A flat, round shellfish found on the sea bed. Oysters are eaten either raw or cooked.

pain au chocolat A sweet breakfast pastry, like a croissant, filled with chocolate.

India

basmati rice A long-grained rice with a nutty flavor and smell.

chapati A round, flat bread made of whole-wheat flour and water. Chapatis are often used to scoop up *dal* and other sauces.

dal Legumes such as lentils or chickpeas cooked with spices and served as a sauce or a soup.

guava A round, yellow-skinned tropical fruit with a strong, sweet smell and pink flesh.

halwa A firm spiced pudding made with semolina flour, sugar, and clarified butter.

papaya A large, pear-shaped tropical fruit with bright yellow skin and smooth yellow flesh.

puri A soft, flat bread that is deep fried until puffy and golden brown.